"1990"

To: Dorine
"The La

In Christian Love,

Reba L. Smith

PATHWAYS OF LIFE THROUGH POETRY

PATHWAYS OF LIFE THROUGH POETRY

Reba L. Smith

VANTAGE PRESS
New York • Los Angeles

FIRST EDITION

Published by Vantage Press, Inc.
516 West 34th Street, New York, New York 10001

Manufactured in the United States of America
ISBN: 0-533-08708-2

Library of Congress Catalog Card No.: 89-90340

1 2 3 4 5 6 7 8 9 0

To my children, Constance Kay Bonardelli and
Jimmy Hugh Gourdie.

Contents

Preface

Getting a book placed on the market has been my dream since high school days. I enjoy my own poetry and have complete faith in it. My dream is to reach out and touch many hearts and to leave an imprint. I have a deep feeling my poems will even change some people's lives. I truly believe the public will enjoy them; some may laugh and some may cry. Each poem has a story to tell within itself.

I was born Reba Leona Gambill in Hymera, Indiana, but moved with my parents and three sisters to Sullivan, Indiana, at the age of six. My father had a small chain of grocery stores in cities and towns nearby.

I graduated from Sullivan High School. All through my school years I went by my middle name, and so my hometown will remember me as Leona Gambill.

Not long after graduating from high school, I came to Davison, Michigan, working for Dr. and Mrs. Del Zingro. There I met my first husband, Hugh Gourdie. This marriage lasted thirty years, and we were the proud parents of a daughter, Constance Kay, and a son, Jim Hugh. When the children were nine and five years of age, I went to work for the GMC Spark Plug Division, where I worked for twenty-one years. Two years after this marriage ended, I married Donald L. Smith. This marriage ended in divorce after six years, but we have remained very good friends. Even to this day we go out to dinner three days a week.

I now live in the small city of Mount Morris, just a few miles north of Flint, Michigan. I am a member of the

United Brethren in Christ Church, which has been a great blessing to me.

I love being with what few loved ones I have near me. I love reading and writing poetry. I enjoy traveling and meeting new people, although I haven't had the chance to do this too much. I enjoy playing the organ, playing cards, crocheting, and keeping house.

I am just a simple person who is quite satisfied with her life. I try not to look back but strive with hope to the future.

Part One

Poems of Everyday Living

Happy Birthday to a Wonderful Daughter

I love you more
   Than words can say
So have yourself
   A most wonderful day.

May the year ahead
   Be ever so bright
Good and gentle
   As soft candlelight.

So always look up
   And don't be forlorn
'Cause I just thank God
   That you were born.

Love,
Mom

Happy Birthday to a Wonderful Son

My son, my son
  How proud I am
That you've grown to be
  Such a fine young man.

Seems like only yesterday
  I wiped away your tears,
Read your favorite stories,
  And spoofed away your fears.

You've given me memories
  And you've made me see
How proud that you are you
  And glad that I am me.

Love,
Mom

Life's Contentment

Snowflakes fell upon her cheek.
  They glistened in her hair.
She looked so bright and cheerful
  As she stood beside me there.

She took my arm so tenderly
  And I walked tall with pride
I had the love I always wanted,
  Walking there by my side.

We walked on softly through the snow,
  Not feeling any of winter's cold.
Love like this is seldom found,
  Such as ours, so I've been told.

I counted my blessings each step I took.
  Truly contented with my life,
You see, this sweet young girl,
  For fifty years, has been my wife.

Floating Lily Pad

I saw a floating lily pad
Come floating down the stream.
If I could but lie upon it
And dream a little dream.

I'd dream about the coming year
And what all we have to face
Then perchance all our troubles
Would fall right into place.

While floating on that lily pad
I'd feel the sunny breeze
Then I'd look around me
And see the beauty of the trees.

Beauty is in the beholder,
It's there for you and I,
So come join me on my lily pad
As I come floating by.

We'd make a wish for all the world
That no one be lonely or sad,
Wish them the happiest year ahead
While floating on our lily pad.

Library of My Mind

I never knew that I would be
What the Master already knew and saw in me.
I took His gifts, so warm and kind
Tucked them away in the library of my mind.

I've risen higher than my expectations,
Been truly blessed with inspirations.
I rummage through memories when I go to find,
Stored away in the library of my mind.

Memories are good. Some are glad,
Some are happy, some are sad.
Throw out the bad, keep those that shine;
This will brighten the library of your mind.

I love my memories; they are part of me
Just as they were meant to be.
Miracles of my life, sealed and signed,
Placed there, in the library of my mind.

Dreams and Hope

We all have dreams,
I'm sure that is true.
Some have so many
Yet others have too few.

I dreamed of having children
And that dream did come true.
I thought of having three,
But was blessed by only two.

I dreamed of writing poetry,
Being the author of many books,
Of being famous some far day
If I was granted the time that it took.

I'd like to think that when I leave
This earthly world behind
I might leave at least one dream
To stir the fantasy of others' minds.

Did You Ever

Did you ever see a baby bird
Learning how to fly?
It didn't quit; it kept on trying
Till it winged high in the sky.

Did you ever see a new spring flower
Bursting into heavenly bloom?
It's trying to tell you at this time
That summer is coming soon.

Did you ever hear some beautiful laughter
Filled with spirit and joy?
Just like the love that is strong
Between a girl and boy?

Did you ever wake on Christmas morn
And thank God for all He has done
And thanked Him that He sacrificed
His only begotten Son?

Did you ever take your parents' hands
And thank them for staying together;
For the love they gave you and security too?
Did you ever? Did you ever?

Graduation Dance

You stood before me and smiled
As you took my hand.
You guided me to the floor
To dance to the band.

I knew you were handsome
As I looked up for a glance,
And you drew me so closely;
'Twas our graduation dance.

As we danced through the night
It was coming to an end
And I knew that my life
Was ready to begin.

You whispered that you loved me
As we glided along.
All these memories I'll cherish
Of a most wonderful prom.

A Home with Love

You can build a home
And fancy it up.
You can buy pretty things,
Maybe cater to a pup.
You can work overtime hours
And money have a lot,
But when you look from the sidelines,
Just what have you got?

For a home is not a home
Without a loving atmosphere;
It takes love, caring and sharing,
And freedom from fear.
It takes much of one's self
For a marriage to survive;
You really must work at it
To keep love alive.

Love needs to be nourished
And it needs to be fed;
It needs the Lord's guidance,
For it needs to be led.
So to have this kind of home,
You need this kind of love;
Surely those that have it
Are blessed from above.

A home should have joy
And laughter in every room,
Just as it was
When you were bride and groom.
So when you build a home,
Build it on solid rock and find,
No matter what the weather or storm,
It will survive the test of time.

My Flowers—My Love

I planted some flowers
The day you went away.
You whispered so softly,
"I'll be back one of these days."

I nurtured those flowers,
For they knew that I cared.
They knew they represented
The love that we shared.

Each day grew to months,
Each month into years;
Yet I knew that my flowers
Each spring would appear.

One day I was awakened
By a knock on my door;
My love had returned
From that faraway war.

We heard a slight noise
As we turned to see
The flowers swaying briskly
In the summer breeze.

They never seemed more beautiful
Or colorful and bright
As we sprinkled them with love
And bid them a good-night.

Fearful Love

I love you, my darling
But I'm stalling for time,
Wanting you to take two steps
To just one of mine.

Why do I do this
When I love you so?
Afraid for my heart?
Afraid to let go?

Wishing and waiting
For you to call,
Yet fearful at the same time
That again I might stall.

Is it all because
My heart has been bruised,
Afraid to let go
And once again I'll refuse?

So come quickly, my darling
And hold me so tight.
Don't let me escape
Into a darkening night.

Just hold me so closely
Till all fears go astray,
Then I can tell you I'm yours
For now, forever, and always.

Why

My darling, my darling,
I love you so much.
If only you were near,
If only we could touch.

Why did you leave me
For that far away land
When we had so many dreams
In the palm of our hands?

I'm sitting here lonely,
Letting time slip away,
Can't seem to adjust
To each heartbreaking day.

Why can't I pull up
From this life of despair
When I know you are watching
And know that you care?

So I went to your room
In the darkness of night
And I found many answers
By dawn's early light.

So now that the answers
Have shown me the way,
I can smile and laugh
At each passing day.

I no longer ask why;
I feel so lifted up
For I know some day
We'll be able to touch.

Just Call Me

Call me if you need me,
For I will never turn you down.
I keep waiting for the phone to ring,
But I never hear a sound.

Please call me if you're lonely
And your pillow is wet from tears.
I'll be waiting to console you,
To chase away all your fears.

Just to hold you in my arms again,
To make old dreams come true;
I know we can find our heaven
And chase away past blues.

So call me and tell me
That you feel the way I do.
Just come home, dear, where you belong
And we'll start our life anew.

Yes, my darling, I still love you.
I'll be waiting right here until
You return to my open arms
For I love you and always will.

A Helping Hand

He found me when I was lonely,
I knew not what to do.
He made things seem so simple
And dark skies turned to blue.

I wanted to hold tight to that moment,
When a helping hand he gave.
It made me feel like standing tall;
It made me feel so very brave.

He made me feel like shouting
To the world so far and wide.
How great it is to have a friend,
A helping hand, there by your side.

Winter and Summer

I jump out of bed
And I pull up the blind.
Now, guess what I see?
The beautiful sunshine.

It has been a long time coming
And far overdue.
Just imagine all our dreams
Of summer fun coming true.

I believe we all lie dormant
As the winter takes its toll,
Yet it gives us all the time we need
To exercise our souls.

Then the clouds roll out to sea,
The sun bursts forth to shine its face,
Which makes me glad that winter comes
So summers can come to take its place.

Precious Friendship

Did I lose something I hold dear,
Or did I misplace it along the way?
Maybe I was careless and knew full well
Friendships don't thrive in hard dry clay.

Maybe we both were careless,
Maybe it gathered with dust,
But it's much too precious to throw aside
And eventually lay to rust.

Let's make it all come true again,
This friendship we once knew.
Never again to be taken for granted,
For friendships are all too few.

We shared so much together,
We bared our hearts and souls.
Let us never again get lost, my friend.
Let us make it our life-long goal.

Yesterday

Back through the years my thoughts do stray
To Christmas times and holidays.
Times were poor and gifts were few,
But how I yearn for yesterday.

Clothes were hanging on the line,
Speckled hens their eggs would lay,
Birds were busy making nests;
Oh, how I yearn for yesterday.

Back through the years my mind does go.
A time to forget about today,
A time to forget what lies ahead,
Just dreaming about our yesterday.

A smokehouse comes to my mind just now
And the smell of fresh mown hay
Sliding down an old barn roof—
This all happened like yesterday.

A schoolhouse just up the alley,
A railroad track not far away.
We could jump rope and hopscotch—
All these bring back memories of yesterday.

It's nice to lie back in your chair
And let your mind stray as it may,
For we had many wonderful years
Made up of many yesterdays.

Part Two

Poems of Love, Caring, and Sharing

My Friend and My Buddy

I've had my dog since his puppy days;
Just a little small ball of fur.
No one seemed to want him
And that's how this all occurred.

Now this little ball of fur
Wrapped himself around my heart
With trusting eyes and mischievous ways
We're seldom ever apart.

He is like my shadow wherever I go.
He guards my home when I'm gone,
He lets me know he loves me
Whether I'm right or maybe wrong.

He's my buddy and always my friend;
The best pal I ever had.
He licks my face to wake me up
And I'm proud to be his dad.

The Way Things Are

I was sitting here, pondering and wondering why
The older we get, how time does fly.
I find myself wishing I could tell time to stop
So I could try and remember everything I forgot.

Either time is going too fast or I'm just too slow.
I'm wondering if I just got here or if it's time to go.
Now with my memory fading and time going fast,
Should I look to my future or continue living in the past?

Now I know many others are affected this way.
They thought it was yesterday when it really was today.
We all sympathized with each other, you see,
And unanimously agreed it was pure misery.

They say all things work together for good,
But I'll never understand this even if I could.
I know I should thank you for setting me straight,
But I'm sorry you did it a little too late.

Just Another Birthday

Another birthday is rolling around
And I'll be sixty-one.
I can't whoop it up as I used to,
But I can still have lots of fun.

I can laugh at my sagging muscles,
I can laugh at my double chin,
I can laugh at the fat I've put on
Where I used to be so thin.

If my bunions hurt and my feet get sore
And I feel rotten right down to the core,
I still won't care what people say.
Just gonna have my fun, anyway.

Who cares if I wear dentures
And there are wrinkles in my scrawny neck?
There is no one knows better than I
That I'm just one old physical wreck.

Yep! I'm gonna laugh at old mother nature,
I'm gonna tell her where to get off
'Cause I'm well over twenty-one now,
And by golly, I'm my own boss!

Retirement Years

Some look upon retirement as the beginning of the end,
Sort of like looking at the downward trend.
But not so, I'm here to say
You are looking at it all the wrong way.

You ask me why I still look young.
Well, it's because retirement can be such fun.
No boss to cater to, no time clock to punch,
No hurrying through a sandwich for your lunch.

We have memories of our childhood,
But the best of them all
Was bringing up our families;
Such sweet memories to recall.

We have grandchildren to cuddle,
We can bounce them on our knee.
Their kisses and hugs are precious
And their fingerprints are free.

No time to sit in a rocking chair.
There is so much to be done,
All those things we couldn't do
Back in the years when we were young.

We can pack our clothes and travel,
See all the beautiful sights,
And we are much too patient and mature
To let petty things cause a fight.

We have time for all our old friends.
We have time to make some new.
Why, we have time for almost everything
And do anything we choose!

I wouldn't trade my life for all the world,
For my golden years are here.
I may have to slow down now and then,
But that's nothing for me to fear.

I look upon my retirement years
As just another life in store,
And if my life here ended tomorrow,
'Twould be just the opening of another door.

Let's Go on a Tour

Are you having a time smiling, my friend
And finding it hard for sleeping?
Well, come along on a tour with me;
You might just end up weeping.

Let's take a tour through the grocery store.
Take along all those coupons, too,
'Cause every nickel and dime will help
Toward paying that bill for you.

On down the aisle we push our carts.
Did you see the price stamped on that bread?
And look at that price hanging over that lettuce
For just one limp, soft head.

It's all too high for my pocketbook,
But I sure need some potatoes.
Well, blow me down! Do you see what they want
For just three scrawny tomatoes!

I don't know what they will come up with next.
They have those no-label cans called generics.
They think they're so smart, so now they come out
With another one called gemerics.

Who gives them the right to treat us like this?
Changing all the prices this way?
Cans with sticker prices atop one another—
Sure wasn't like that yesterday.

I finally made it to the check-out counter.
I'm feeling sick down to the core.
Then they hand me a long slip of paper
Just before I head for the door.

They say food prices were way down this month,
But it's not so when I go to pay
'Cause when I get home, I say to myself,
"Lady, you've had one hell of day!"

Part Three

Poems to Make You Laugh

Ice Cream and Tartar Sauce

My friend and I heard of this brand new restaurant
That just opened in our beautiful mall,
So we got in the car and drove right over
To give this place a call.

Now, let me tell you about this place,
Restaurants like these are mighty few;
The food revolved around in a circle—
You didn't walk to it, the food came to you.

Now we stood there taking some of this and that;
It all looked mighty good.
Our plates were running out of room;
There was food on top of food.

All we wanted to do was sample
A little bit of it all,
So we finally took another plate.
By cracky, we were having a ball!

We sauntered over to the other bar
Where the dessert came with the meal.
We got us some strawberry shortcake
With flowing ice cream—boy what a deal!

Time we got to our table
With all that food piled high,
We both knew our stomachs
Were much smaller than our eyes.

Well, I finally made it to my dessert.
Then I knew I'd been double-crossed,
'Cause what I thought was vanilla pudding
Turned out to be tartar sauce.

But worst of all was when I saw
That pretty ice cream running across,
Just like a beautiful stream
Right into that darn tartar sauce.

One thing I learned: When I go to this place
I'm gonna let my stomach be boss,
'Cause never in the world will I learn to like
Ice cream and tartar sauce!

Excuses

Someday I'm going to invent
A clock that just tells time.
No pesty alarm to disturb my sleep,
So, Lord, I must decline.

I worked hard all week, my Lord,
And I deserve my rest.
You have no idea what I've been through,
But next Sunday I'll try my best.

I kept on making excuses
As that alarm kept blasting away.
The Lord just doesn't seem to understand
Anything or any word I say.

So, pastor, you sing your song about excuses
And I'll read this little poem.
But the fear of God has been put in me,
So guess it's time I got goin'.

So the following week I went to church
And I opened up its door.
I sang, "Let's Forget About Ourselves and Magnify Our
Lord."
And you know what? I'm not sleepy anymore.

Kidding with the Lord

Lord, would you mind if I draw closer to Thee
To have a long talk—just you and me?
There are questions galore I want answers to,
And I want the answers while talking to you.

Why, Lord? Why can't I stay young?
Growing old, you know, isn't much fun.
I look in the mirror and wrinkles I see,
And sagging muscles down to my knees.

Why, Lord? Why are you laughing at me
When I take these things so seriously?
I've a kink in my neck and an ache in my head
And my back aches so, I feel half dead.

Well, Lord, I know you've things to do.
You knew all along I was kidding with you,
But hasn't it been fun fellowshiping this way?
What a great way to end the day!

Oh, wait, Lord, wait. Help me up off my knees;
Been on them so long, they're stiff, you see.
Just point me in the direction where I'll find my bed.
Enough is enough, whatever I said.

Good night, Lord.

Big Toe and I

"Good morning," I said to my old big toe.
"Just what have you got in store for me today?"
I talk harshly to my ugly old toe,
'Cause we've never gotten along good anyway.

I opened up the icebox
For some orange juice to start my day.
And don't you know when I slammed the door,
That old big toe got in the way.

I shook my finger at big old toe
"Just what have I ever done to you?
You're not happy looking like my other toes;
You've got to be black and blue."

Months went by and I said to big toe,
"We've got to make amends."
So I took a hammer and let him have it.
Since then, we've been the best of friends.

Part Four

Poems of Spiritual Value

An Easter Wish

Easter is a lovely time
To write a poem to you
To tell you what you mean to me,
For true friends are mighty few.

Friendship is a gift from God
Given only from above.
He knew we needed each other
So he did it through His love.

You have put many a smile upon my face
And sunshine in my heart.
You've made me sing with laughter,
Even though we may be apart.

So, my friend, it means a lot
To know you think of me.
Friendship ties are precious bonds
Like a life long family tree.

So I am wishing you an Easter
That's as bright as it can be
And your hopes and dreams will all come true
For you and your family.

"Glory Be to God—Give Thanks unto Him"

During this busy season, let us keep our minds on Him and give thanks to a big and wonderful God. Our God is full of love, peace, and mercy. He is so faithful. He is our strength and power, our fortress, our resting place. He is victory.

Let us pause and give thanks for the free country where we are privileged to live. Let us give thanks for our wonderful church, our pastor and his family, and all those that give of their time and service. Let us give thanks for all that He has done in and for us this past year.

> "In the beginning was the Word, and the Word was with God, and the Word was God."

After all is said and done, we know the best is yet to come.

Happy Thanksgiving Day

O Holy Night

Jesus was born on a beautiful night.
The star in the east was shining so bright.
The wise men were searching the King of the Jews
They kneeled and worshipped the blessed news.

They traveled far and rejoiced with great joy
As they laid eyes on the precious little boy.
Mary was smiling while holding God's Son,
For she knew she had born the Holy One.

Let us all worship Him this Christmas Season.
Knowing Jesus is really the only true reason
That we celebrate with such love and care,
And all that we have, we're willing to share.

May we all have faith, peace and love,
Thank Him for being heirs to His kingdom above.
Enjoy your Christmas Day right down to the end
With all your loved ones, neighbors, and friends.

Merry Christmas
and a Wonderful
Year Ahead

Looking Forward with Hope

Thank you, Lord, for this brand new year
That Thou has given to me.
May it be full of spirit and joy
And many a soul set free.

Oh blessed Lord, I love you so
How great Thou art to me
You took my heart right from the start
Because of Calvary.

May I use this year to seek and find
Through Your scriptures so true and wise.
And bind and brand them in my heart
So they'll be easy to recognize.

Now when I go to draw on them,
To help a friend in need,
I will only have to go and pluck,
To plant another seed.

Now in this year of eighty-nine
I'll need much meditation
To help me strive for higher ground
For an eternal celebration.

Those stepping stones so hard to climb
To that stairway in the sky,
Please grant me strength, oh, God, I pray
Until the day I die.

Happy New Year

Part Five

Spiritual Poetry to Awaken and Stir Your Heart

Come to the Altar

If you feel a need for peace within,
Come to the altar and meet your friend.
Oh child of God, He is waiting for you,
He will comfort, bless you, and make you new.

He will cast your sins down deep in the sea.
He will break the chains and set you free.
Just call Him Lord and repent of your sins,
Then, all of a sudden, your new life begins.

He will help you to grow and pave your way.
The Holy Spirit He will give to counsel your days.
Because you met Him at the altar today, my friend,
Much more will he give you for forgiveness of sin.

Amen

Soul Set Free

This fast life we live today
Is really getting me down
So I packed some food and blankets
And I headed out of town.

There is so much I want to do,
So much I want to see,
So I headed out to the country
To let my soul run free.

"No need to hurry," I told myself.
"Just take your time—don't run."
So I climbed the highest hilltop
To watch the setting sun.

What awesome shadows the sun did make,
Beautiful colors in different shades.
I felt so peaceful with myself
As the sun lowered and began to fade.

Then over yonder I looked to see
A bright full moon so big and round.
Then I closed my eyes and listened
To God's creatures making different sounds.

I fell asleep there on that hill.
Awakened by the leaves on the trees,
They seemed to be whispering, "Why are you here?"
I answered, "Just letting my soul run free."

My House of Worship

When I walk into my house of worship,
See those smiling faces all around,
Precious Lord, you need not tell me
I know I'm walking on holy ground.

A hearty welcome—an extended hand
Just fills my heart with joy.
And I know You're looking from Your throne
In all Your finest glory.

Thank You, Father, for this day set aside
To hear Your word and to absorb,
To sing and praise and worship Thee,
To glorify my precious Lord.

A Visit to Church

They say that going to Sunday School
Is good for heart and soul.
They say to make the church a rule
And look forward to your goal.

We seated ourselves and sang some songs
That neither of us knew,
For we haven't been to church for years.
Sounds awful, but it's true.

Sunday School class was next in line.
Someone was asked to pray,
Verses were read, and my turn came,
But my tongue got in the way.

They gave us each a little book,
We knew not where to turn.
We shuffled through its pages
But nothing did we learn.

We glanced back over our shoulder
At the lady sitting there.
Thought maybe she would help us out,
But she didn't seem to care.

They started asking questions
About God's commandments, love, and law,
About the good-neighbor policy,
And others I can't recall.

So just one thing before I close
About us creatures full of fear:
May God have mercy on our souls
That visit church but once a year.

My Walk with Jesus

Come walk with me, dear Jesus.
Please take me by the hand.
Let me pour out my heartaches
For I know you'll understand.

I know that you will listen
For I know that you care
And I know that my burdens
You're willing to share.

Oh, Lord, I'm so lonely
I can't seem to adjust.
I miss my life's partner,
I miss him so much.

He left such a vacuum
I can't seem to fill.
Yet he left such sweet memories,
I remember them still.

I'll always remember
The things that he said.
The way that he walked,
The books that he read.

I can see him going fishing,
Maybe fixing a kite,
And I can hear him still whisper
A gentle good-night.

But now that he's left me
I'm trying to adjust.
You tell me I can
And I know that I must.

I feel so much better
Just walking with you,
And I know you will guide me
In all that I do.

So why am I weary
And why do I fret?
For I know life for me
Is not over with yet.

Thank you, dear Jesus,
For being so strong
And letting me lean
On Thee for so long.

I know when my life
On earth for me is o'er,
I know that I'll meet him
On life's other shore.

My Rebirth in Christ

It came to me suddenly, one long gloomy day,
That life wasn't all it should be.
I thought and I studied and finally knew
There was something lacking in me.

I felt sort of lonely, I felt sort of blue.
I felt life passing me by.
Then all of a sudden I knew what it was,
And I took a deep breath and a sigh.

"I need a friend," I said to myself.
One that's true as could be.
One I could count on through thick and through thin
And one who could count also on me.

So I prayed to my Lord for just such a friend.
How deeply I prayed for so long.
'Twas over a year I hoped and I prayed,
Then He answered my prayer like a song.

He crossed my path with another,
A friend from long years from the past.
Then I knew the good Lord had answered my prayers.
Yes, He answered my prayers at last.

How grateful I was, how precious it felt
No word could ever express.
No more would I cry in the darkness at night,
No more would I feel so depressed.

But the good Lord knew more than I did;
He knew of my truest need
So He used my true friend down deep in my heart
And there she grew like a seed.

They worked together on me from the start.
At last I could see the light.
No longer did I walk in darkness and despair;
Everything was shiny and bright.

I opened my heart and my sins fell away,
And Jesus came into my heart.
How precious and wonderful and blessed it was.
I now, too, knew what I needed from the start.

What a memorable day, I shall never forget.
'Twas November 3, 1974.
'Twas my mother's birthday, God rest her soul.
For blessings I couldn't ask more.

I've many to thank for their prayers and their deeds
And thanks to our Lord up above
For the greatest of gifts—the greatest of all—
The gift to love and be loved.

So now He leads me by day and by night.
How grateful I always shall be
To my friend, my Jesus and God up above.
And to think this could happen to me!

Looking to Thee

I look to Thee for my every need.
You never let me down,
You lift me up with tender love.
Then all is well, I've found.

My heart feels heavyladen
My heart lays full of pain,
And so I kneel beside my bed
And go to you again.

You show me how to help myself,
You lead me in mysterious ways.
Telling me to take one day at a time
So my hand goes up in praise.

So going to Thee for all my needs
Lightens my heavy load.
The rocky road ahead of me
Turned out to be a simple winding road.

The Mighty Power of Prayer

I had worked so hard for others
Each day the whole week long.
I did not mind, I just was tired.
My energy I thought was gone.

I sat there feeling weary
As I lay back in my chair.
Thought I'd ask my Master's help
For I know He always cares.

Before I could ask, the telephone rang,
A voice came over the line.
"How are you feeling today, my friend?"
I said, "I guess I'm feeling fine."

"That's good," she said, "for I need a favor.
I need you to help me out."
But feeling as I did right then,
I really had some doubts.

"What is it, my friend, what do you want?"
She said, "I need you to pray for me."
When she told me all about it,
I was down on bended knee.

While I was asking help for her
He also was helping me
For no longer did I feel so weary
'Twas such a mystery.

Mysterious things do happen.
In this I have no doubt.
Any friend who needs this favor
It's such a pleasure to help them out.

The Miracle of God

When I went seeking my Savior one day
I found Him there waiting and let Him have His way.
I cried out my heartache for forgiveness of sin.
My heart lay wide open, please Jesus come in.

I asked for atonement, for blood that He shed.
He just smiled at me, not a word was said.
Such peace that came on me, I'll never forget
And how my life changed, I can remember it yet.

I told my Dear Savior, "In You I believe.
Believe that you died. You rose and are coming for me.
I believe in my Father, the Master of us all
He is there to support us, He won't let us fall."

I knew a big change in my life had to be.
To walk with my Jesus was worth it, you see.
So long did I ponder and long did I pray
And clearly I saw He is the Truth, the Life, and the Way.

It hasn't been easy, there are times I've been blue.
The road up ahead looks so lonely, too.
Then I looked up and saw His dear, sweet face
And thanked my Dear God for giving me grace.

So late that day as I knelt by my bed,
In the quietness and darkness I heard what He said.
"Have patience, my child and you will see
The promise of my Father will set you free."

Through all of the heartaches and burdens to bare,
We've grown so much closer, for I know He cares.
There is a fountain of strength we can draw from above
With it comes peace, coupled with love.

"For ask it of Me, in His Holy name
And it shall be given, for you're not ashamed.
You have proven yourself through word and through deed
Glory be yours and you shall I lead."

The change in my life has now come about,
But in this, dear Lord, I now have no doubt.
And now each day, I'll be able to say,
"Thank You, dear God, for doing it Your way."

Reaching Out in Space

If I could just reach out in space
And touch the hand I used to know,
I'd grasp it tightly and lean your way
To tell you how much I love you so.

But time passes on and now we are parted,
So now what can I say?
The vacuum in my heart is there
And I know it's there to stay.

We never planned our lives would be
Ever for us to part,
But we parted in different directions
And both with broken hearts.

I use to see you from time to time.
You looked so lonely and blue,
But you never knew down deep inside
How lonely I was, too.

It is best I not look backward,
Just to live from day to day,
But that road ahead looks rocky
When you are alone on life's pathway.

But alone I must go and travel on
And make the best of things,
To take whatever life has for me
No matter what it brings.

It's surely not easy growing old alone,
It's like nothing I can describe.
The emptiness of it all, you see,
There's no one by your side.

I must not cry, I must be brave
For now you have found your resting place,
But in my heart I shall always carry
The picture of your dear, sweet face.

Who knows what life may have in store
Or what God has already planned?
Maybe someday we will meet again,
Then I can reach out and touch your hand.

He Is There

If ever you think that things get rough
And life is hard to bear
Just cast your eyes upward
And you'll see Him watching there.

He never misses anything,
He sees all there is to see
So if you feel you are overburdened
Just drop it and let it be.

For He will gladly take them from you
And cast them far astray
If only you will ask Him
In a sweet and childlike way.

He is so sweet and generous,
Loving, compassionate, and kind.
So never close your eyes at night
Until He is on your mind.

Just praise Him and love Him,
Show Him that you care.
Then life will take on new meaning
And it won't be so hard to bear.

Just keep on looking upward
Cast your eyes into the sky.
For He is there, the one we know
Who died for you and I.

Four Roses on the Vine

Four roses grew
Upon the vine.
Three were my sisters',
The other was mine.

We blossomed and grew
Ever so tall and fine.
We loved the outdoors
With the sun upon the vine.

We grew and multiplied
Each in our own direction.
The wind blew up together at times.
Oh what a great reflection!

The Lord was kind to us
Through rough times and the good.
He made us nice and strong,
So through the storms we understood.

We went through the colds of winters
Through the snow, sleet, and hail,
But then would come the sunshine.
Lord, we knew you wouldn't fail.

Then one terrible day did come,
One branch of the vine was snipped away.
It left us other roses still standing.
We dropped our heads and prayed.

We shall cherish every memory
Of the rose that used to be,
For we know within our hearts
She is resting there with Thee.

So on we go to further heights.
We question not what lies in store,
For only Thee, we know, sweet Lord,
Knows the name on the coming door.

Three Roses on the Vine

The vine is still growing,
But Lord, just today,
The second of four roses
Has been snipped away.

My heart is so heavy,
I miss them so much,
But I know they are where
They have Your gentle touch.

Now there are just two roses left,
One my sister's, one is mine.
We must continue to grow
In the rain and sunshine.

The oldest and the youngest
Are the ones that remain,
And I know it will never
Ever be quite the same.

My Lord, you've taken them so far away,
These two dear sisters of mine,
Where once we used to be so close
Growing so proudly on the vine.

I really do understand, dear Lord.
I understand it all:
That once given life upon the vine
Eventually we must fall.

May Thy goodness and grace be with us
As You grant us strength for each day.
May You and Your Holy Spirit keep us strong
Until You come to take us away.

My Sister

Dear Lord, I thank you for all blessings
And Your word I do proclaim.
Hear my prayer, oh Lord, how grateful I am
That I have one sister who remains.

This sister means so much to me,
It's hard for words to express.
But knowing through Thy grace and power,
I feel so truly blessed.

We go through life and give so little.
We rarely stop to think,
That as the wheels of life keep turning,
You may take away the missing link.

For Thou art all powerful and mighty
And through Thee all blessings flow.
We'd have it no other way, my Lord.
Through Thy lessons we gracefully grow.

So now I thank you, once again
That you've reached down and touched
And blessed me with a dear sweet sister
Whom I love so very much.

I Do Not Need to See His Face

Though I've never seen Him, I love Him;
Though I've never seen Him, I believe in Him.
He is everywhere I see and touch.
That is why I love Him so much.

I see Him in a child's sweet face;
I feel Him in all His goodness and grace;
I see Him in the birds and trees;
I feel His presence when I'm on my knees.

I do not need to prove my faith;
I see Him all over the place,
Just like the rivers that go flowing by,
Just as the stars that light the sky.

All these things I do believe
And thank Him for things I've achieved.
I patiently wait to take His hand
And gently be lead to that Promised Land.

Guide Me, Lord

Guide me, Lord, today I pray
That I might plant a seed today.
For tomorrow, my Lord, may be too late.
I so want to do this for your sake.

Guide me, Lord, by Thy mighty hand
That the valleys in my life I'll understand,
To bear the pain and all the sorrow
Knowing the sun will shine tomorrow.

Guide me, Lord, to be so wise
To the needs of others I'll recognize,
To pray with them and do my best,
To let them know God will do the rest.

Guide me, Lord, by Thy mighty power.
When the countdown comes to the final hour
"Come in child," I'll hear Thee say,
"Your mansion is ready for you to stay."

I Have a Dream

You know, Lord, I have a dream.
I have such hope in my heart
I never would have made it this past year
If I'd never known You from the start.

Yes, I have a dream, Lord
And it means so much to me.
I've pondered and studied and thought it all out
And talked it over with Thee.

I prayed for patience and strength, O God.
I've learned to wait and be still
And I only want this dream of mine
If it be according to Thy will.

I do so want this brand new life,
This brand new place where
I can sing and laugh and enjoy living,
For I know I am needed there.

To be loved, wanted, and needed,
To serve, to help, and to share,
To let your friend and neighbor know
That you truly and sincerely care.

But if by chance Your plans for me
Are not the same as mine,
Though tears may flow, I'll still pray,
"Please grant me the test of time."

Thank you for being so generous and kind,
For all Your goodness and grace.
And when I close my eyes tonight
May I see Your dear, sweet face.

Healing Praise

In the stillness, darkness, and peace of the night
I've come to praise Your name.
I've come to Your throne of glory,
Knowing You will always be the same.

I'm so grateful I've come to know You
And to know the power of prayer.
How else can I reach you, my Master,
And to know how deeply You care?

So I told You of my plight—the suffering and pain.
I felt no relief was in sight,
Yet I told you of my faith
And you healed me that beautiful night.

Praise be unto Thee, my Lord,
And praise Thee for showing to me
How great Thou art through mercy and grace.
I praise Thee for healing me.

Truly Grateful

I love to talk to my Father.
He's always there for me,
And when I go to talk with Him
I know right where He'll be.

I'm so grateful, precious Jesus,
That you shed your blood for me
That I might have life everlasting
When You died on Calvary.

I'm grateful for the reading of Your word,
The time and closeness that we share,
So grateful that we can communicate
Through the wonderful power of prayer.

I'm grateful You warned me of Satan
And told me of his wicked ways.
Now I know when I hear the true word
I can stand firm on all You say.

I'm grateful for the peace I feel within.
The Holy Spirit guides me thus.
With the filling and cleansing, my soul's engraved
With the words, "In God I Trust."

Our Creator Gave

You gave us this most beautiful and wonderful land,
Which you made by your great and mighty hand
You gave us the sky to light our way
You gave us night and gave us the day.

You gave us oceans, lakes, and streams,
You gave so much to fulfill our dreams.
You gave us cattle and fruit-bearing trees,
And food from the waters to supply our needs.

You gave ways to multiply and have dominion over all.
You gave us valleys and mountains so tall,
You gave us all winged birds and much good seed.
All this you gave through Thy mighty deeds.

Then you gave us a day to rest and rejoice
And left it to us to make the right choice.
Then you gave us Your only begotten Son
That through Him we might enter your divine kingdom.

Glory be to God.

I'm Going Home

An angel appeared at my bedside last night,
Told me my time was growing nigh.
Said I'd been chosen; I must go
To my home up in the sky.

Then Jesus appeared beside my bed.
He laid His hands on me.
He said it's time to come and live
With Him eternally.

Just remember the memories of love we shared
And remember I'm happy to be
The mother of three beautiful children
Who brought much comfort and joy to me.

Please don't grieve too long for me.
You all must realize
We'll meet again, some far day
In this home called Paradise.

Fond Farewell

A fond farewell I say to you
With a slight wave of the hand.
I've been chosen—I must go
To that beautiful Promised Land.

So please don't weep and hurt too long.
I'm going to where the angels sing their songs,
Where I can rest and be in peace,
Where joy and laughter will never cease.

Remember the memories of love we shared
And remember I'm happy to be
The mother of two beautiful children
A son, Jimmy, and a daughter, Connie.

A fond farewell to all of you.
I've found my resting place
Where I can walk on golden streets
And look upon my Savior's face.